EYES

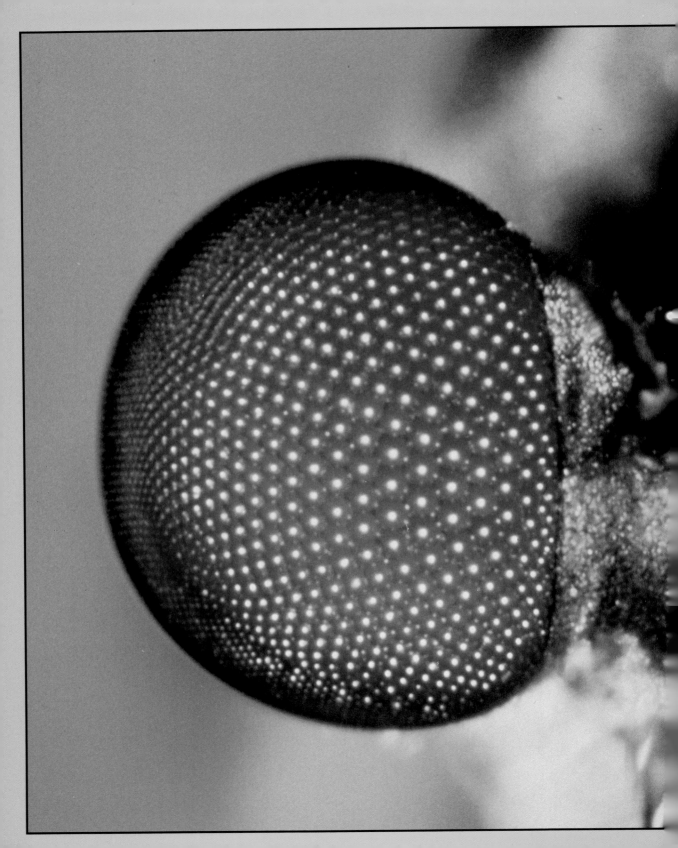

Picture Credits
Stephen J. Krasemann/DRK: cover
G & R Grambo: pages 8, 10, 11, 17
Steve Satushek/Image Bank: page 6
Dwight Kuhn: pages 15, 16-17, 24
Zig Leszczynski: pages 9, 22, 27
Mary Beth Angelo/Photo Researchers: page 25
Secret Sea Visions: page 18
A.B. Sheldon: pages 7, 12
Marty Snyderman: pages 20
Lynn M. Stone: pages 11, 12, 14
Bill Beatty/Visuals Unlimited: page 23
Arthur B. Hill/Visuals Unlimited: page 8
Kjell B. Sandved/Visuals Unlimited: Endpages; pages 7, 14, 17, 18, 19, 21
Richard Walters/Visuals Unlimited: page 6
Rick and Mora Bowers/Wildlife Collection: page 29
Tom DiMauro/Wildlife Collection: page 29
Michael Francis/Wildlife Collection: page 16
D. Robert Franz/Wildlife Collection: page 13
John Giustina/Wildlife Collection: page 11
Martin Harvey/Wildlife Collection: pages 13, 23, 26
Richard Herrmann/Wildlife Collection: page 22
Chris Huss/Wildlife Collection: page 25
Joe McDonald/Wildlife Collection: pages 20-21
Clay Myers/Wildlife Collection: page 25
B. Stein/Wildlife Collection: page 28

wm
573.88
Gram
16.25

Published by Rourke Publishing LLC

Copyright © 2002 Kidsbooks, Inc.

Printed in the USA

Grambo, Rebecca
  Eyes / Rebecca L. Grambo
      p. cm – (Amazing Animals)
      ISBN 1-58952-144-5

EYES

WRITTEN BY
REBECCA L. GRAMBO

Rourke Publishing LLC
Vero Beach, Florida 32964
rourkepublishing.com

ANIMAL EYES

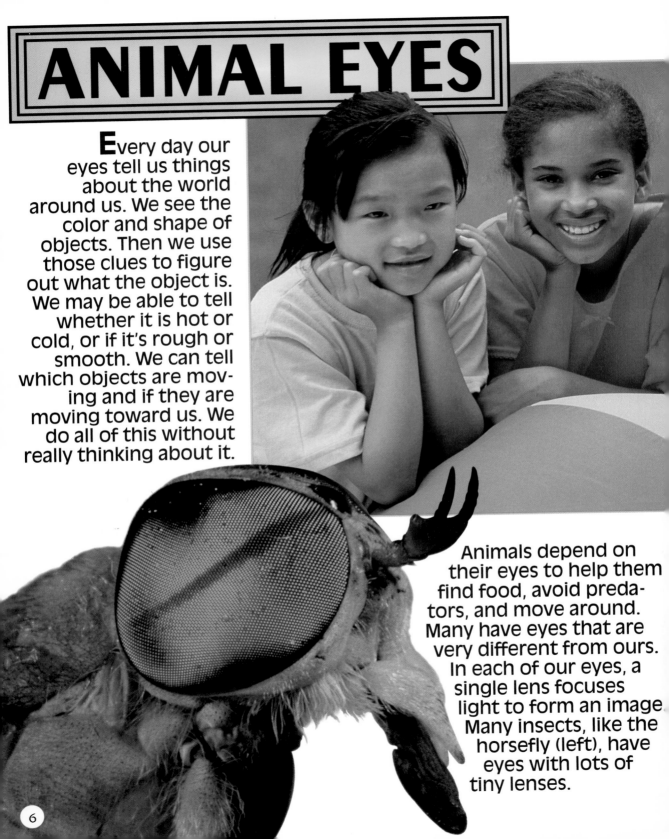

Every day our eyes tell us things about the world around us. We see the color and shape of objects. Then we use those clues to figure out what the object is. We may be able to tell whether it is hot or cold, or if it's rough or smooth. We can tell which objects are moving and if they are moving toward us. We do all of this without really thinking about it.

Animals depend on their eyes to help them find food, avoid predators, and move around. Many have eyes that are very different from ours. In each of our eyes, a single lens focuses light to form an image. Many insects, like the horsefly (left), have eyes with lots of tiny lenses.

A scallop may have as many as 100 tiny eyes. They are scattered in the fringe of tentacles around the shell. Each eye is only about the thickness of a dime! Scallop eyes don't form clear pictures, but they are very good at seeing movement. When a scallop sees a predator coming toward it, the scallop snaps its shell shut!

Most spiders have six or eight eyes. The wolf spider uses all eight of its eyes to hunt for prey. The small eyes on the sides of its head spot movement. Then the spider turns to face its prey so that it can focus with its main eyes and pounce.

IN THE DARK

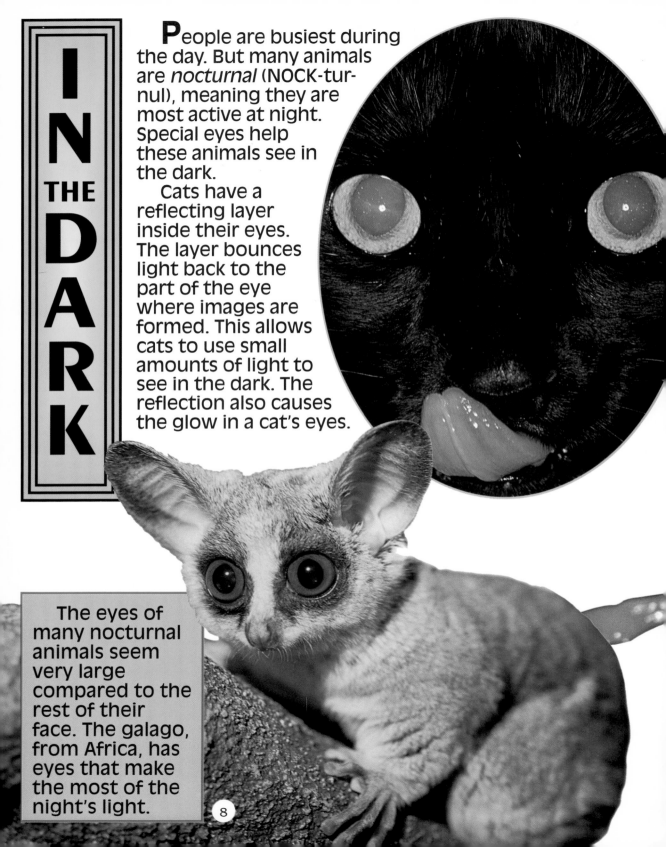

People are busiest during the day. But many animals are *nocturnal* (NOCK-tur-nul), meaning they are most active at night. Special eyes help these animals see in the dark.

Cats have a reflecting layer inside their eyes. The layer bounces light back to the part of the eye where images are formed. This allows cats to use small amounts of light to see in the dark. The reflection also causes the glow in a cat's eyes.

The eyes of many nocturnal animals seem very large compared to the rest of their face. The galago, from Africa, has eyes that make the most of the night's light.

At the center of our eyes, and the eyes of many animals, are small dark openings called *pupils.* They control how much light gets into the eye. Pupils open wide in the dark and close tightly in bright light. Nocturnal animals have very sensitive eyes. They need pupils that can shut tightly during the day. The long, slit pupils of these tree frogs block out bright daylight that could hurt their eyes.

EYES OF THE HUNTER

Our eyes are close together in the front of our head. Cover one eye, then the other. What you see with your right eye overlaps what you see with your left eye. Your brain combines these two images into a three-dimensional picture. This lets you judge how far you are from the objects you are seeing. This is called *binocular* (by–NOK–you–ler) vision. Predators like the wolf, which hunt other animals, usually have eyes positioned the same way as ours.

A cougar uses sight more than its other senses to find food. Once it spots prey, the cougar sneaks closer until it is near enough to attack. Then the cougar's keen vision helps it to time its pounce correctly.

An eagle's eyesight may be as much as eight times better than ours. That means an eagle soaring above a mountain valley may be able to see a rabbit from up to two miles away!

Owls are nocturnal animals that hunt mostly at night and see very well in low light. Owls use their binocular vision to find a scurrying mouse and then— SWOOP!

LOOK OUT!

Some animals are often hunted for food by other animals. To avoid being eaten, these prey animals need to be constantly aware of what's happening around them.

The large eyes of the prairie dog and the deer are placed on the sides of their head. This makes them very good at spotting even slight movement off to the side. They can see approaching predators in time to run away.

The eyes of a bittern are positioned very far apart. To have binocular front vision, the bittern has to point its beak up and look out from underneath it. Another bird, the snipe, has eyes placed way back. It actually has binocular vision behind its head!

Members of the rabbit and hare families can see almost directly behind them. This can be dangerous because it creates a blind spot directly in front of them. One hare was seen running over a cliff because it was so busy watching the predator chasing it!

BUG-EYED

Many insect eyes have lots of tiny lenses called *facets* (FAH–sets). This kind of eye is called a *compound* eye. Compound eyes look very different from our eyes, and they don't form images the same way our eyes do.

Have you ever tried to swat a fly and missed? Compound eyes like those of this robber fly are much better than ours at noticing motion. The fly sees the swatter coming in plenty of time to get out of the way!

The praying mantis is a fierce hunter of other insects. It sees very well, but only within a short distance. Our eyes adjust to focus on distant objects. If an insect with compound eyes wants a better look at something far away, the insect has to move closer.

A dragonfly's eye may have 28,000 to 30,000 facets! Each facet sends back its view of the surrounding scene. The dragonfly sees a picture that is sharp in all directions. Dragonflies have some of the best overall eyesight in the animal kingdom.

CLEVER PUPILS

Animals have pupils of many different shapes. We have round pupils that control the amount of light entering our eyes. Our pupils let in enough light to form an image but not enough to hurt our eyes. As you already know, cats and many other nocturnal animals have pupils shaped like narrow slits.

Members of the gecko family have weird, wavy pupils. They may look fancy but they do the same job as our plain, round ones. Our pupils shrink to smaller circles on a sunny day. In bright light, a gecko's pupil closes down to a number of very small, black dots.

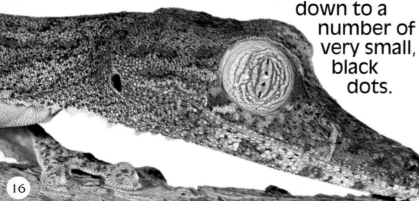

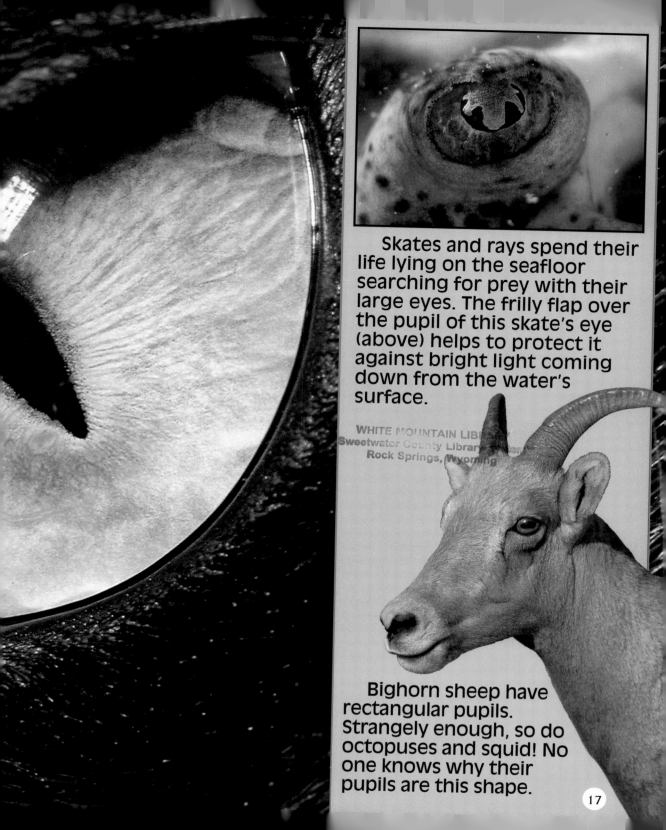

Skates and rays spend their life lying on the seafloor searching for prey with their large eyes. The frilly flap over the pupil of this skate's eye (above) helps to protect it against bright light coming down from the water's surface.

Bighorn sheep have rectangular pupils. Strangely enough, so do octopuses and squid! No one knows why their pupils are this shape.

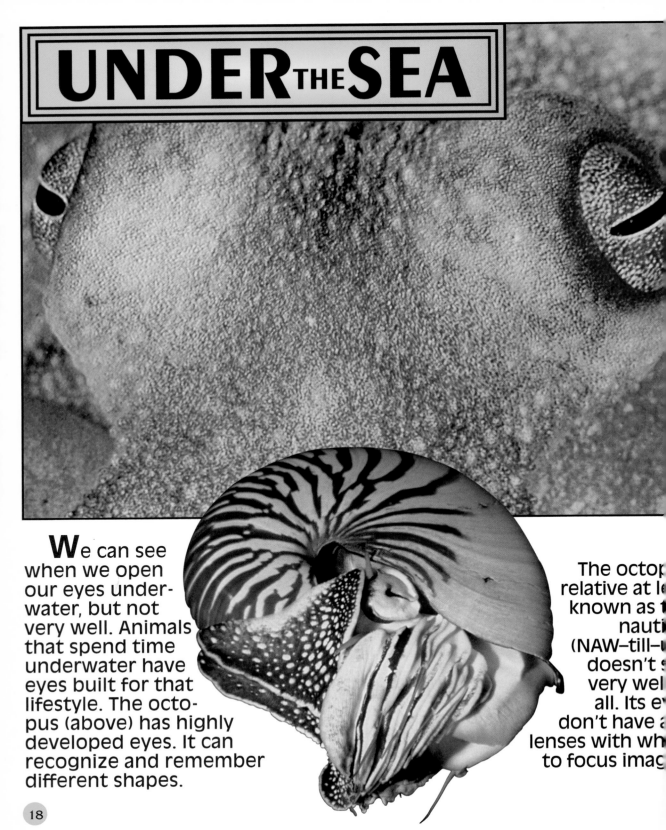

UNDER THE SEA

We can see when we open our eyes under-water, but not very well. Animals that spend time underwater have eyes built for that lifestyle. The octopus (above) has highly developed eyes. It can recognize and remember different shapes.

The octop relative at l known as nauti (NAW–till– doesn't very wel all. Its e don't have lenses with wh to focus imag

Penguins spend much of their time underwater. They see better there than on land. Penguins also have a special third eyelid that covers their eyes when they dive. It protects their eyes and still lets them see the fish they're chasing.

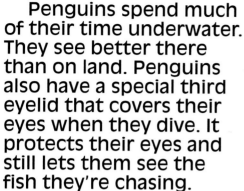

The eyes of the hammerhead shark, as well as its nostrils, are located on the ends of its strangely shaped head. No one knows why. These sharks see well to the sides but have a large blind spot directly in front of them. To see ahead, a hammerhead must swing its head back and forth.

PUT A LID ON IT!

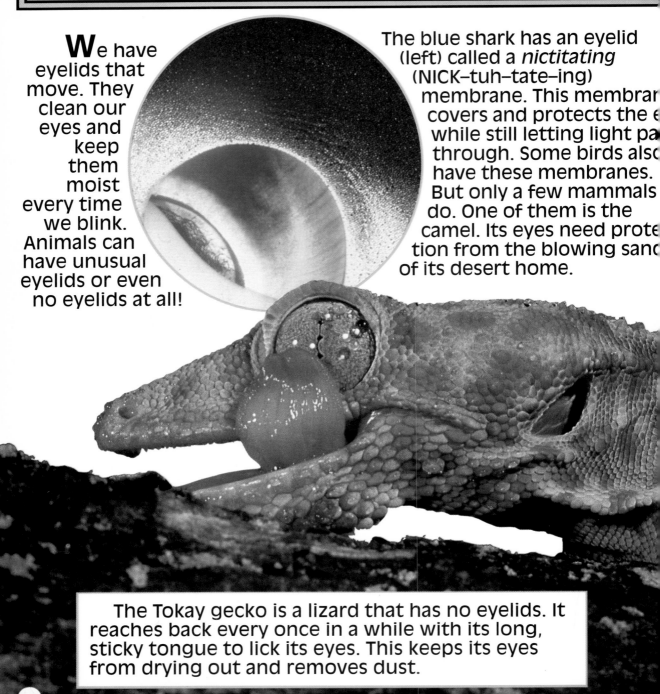

We have eyelids that move. They clean our eyes and keep them moist every time we blink. Animals can have unusual eyelids or even no eyelids at all!

The blue shark has an eyelid (left) called a *nictitating* (NICK–tuh–tate–ing) membrane. This membrane covers and protects the eye while still letting light pass through. Some birds also have these membranes. But only a few mammals do. One of them is the camel. Its eyes need protection from the blowing sand of its desert home.

The Tokay gecko is a lizard that has no eyelids. It reaches back every once in a while with its long, sticky tongue to lick its eyes. This keeps its eyes from drying out and removes dust.

When the sun is very bright, seeing can be difficult. This is a special problem for insects with big eyes and no eyelids. Some insects, like the butterfly at left, have hairs growing in their compound eyes. Scientists think the hairs may help to reduce glare—the same thing sunglasses do for people!

FOOLED YOU!

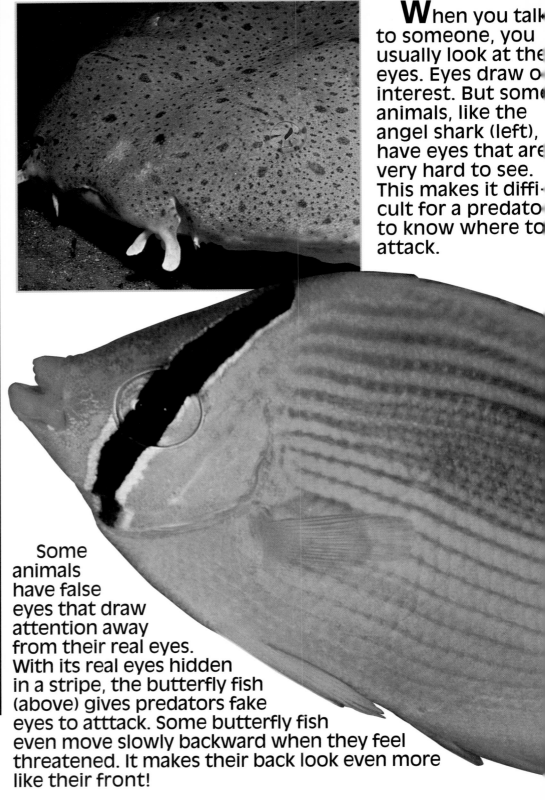

When you talk to someone, you usually look at the eyes. Eyes draw our interest. But some animals, like the angel shark (left), have eyes that are very hard to see. This makes it difficult for a predator to know where to attack.

Some animals have false eyes that draw attention away from their real eyes. With its real eyes hidden in a stripe, the butterfly fish (above) gives predators fake eyes to atttack. Some butterfly fish even move slowly backward when they feel threatened. It makes their back look even more like their front!

The emperor moth suddenly opens its wings to show false eyespots. This might scare or puzzle a predator.

The eyespots on the rear end of this caterpillar certainly might confuse an attacking bird. The spots also draw attention away from the caterpillar's head.

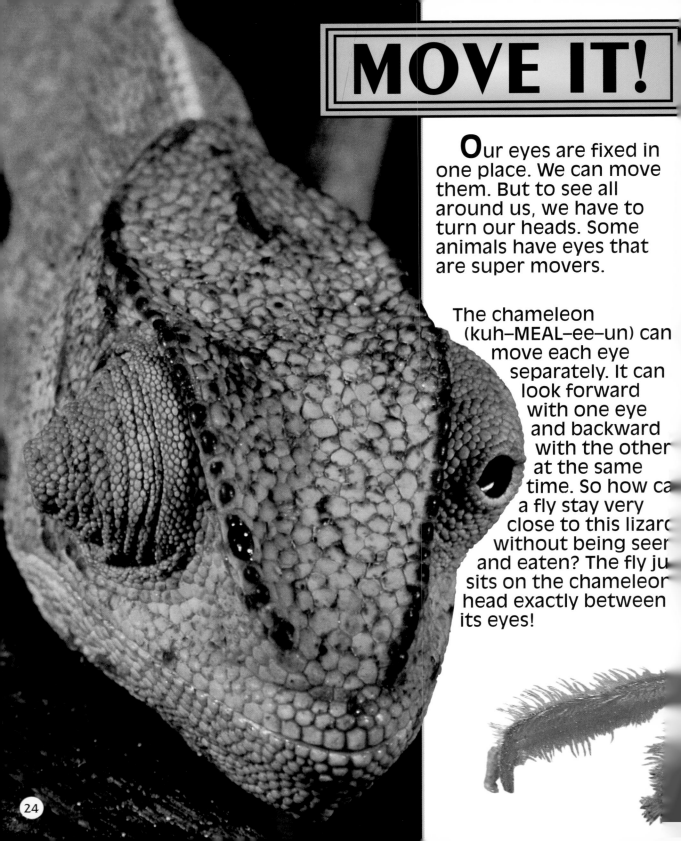

MOVE IT!

Our eyes are fixed in one place. We can move them. But to see all around us, we have to turn our heads. Some animals have eyes that are super movers.

The chameleon (kuh–MEAL–ee–un) can move each eye separately. It can look forward with one eye and backward with the other at the same time. So how ca a fly stay very close to this lizard without being seen and eaten? The fly ju sits on the chameleon head exactly between its eyes!

A flounder's eyes move, but it takes a long time. And it only happens once in the fish's lifetime. When the flounder is small, it looks like any other fish. It has one eye on each side of its head.

But as the flounder grows, something strange begins to happen. One eye very slowly moves across the flounder's head toward the other side of its face. Eventually, both eyes are on one side. The flounder (left) spends its adult life lying on the ocean bottom with its "eye side" up.

The eyes of the conch (KAHNK) and the ghost crab are at the end of movable stalks. The conch (right) is like a big snail. It can pull its eyes back into the protection of its big, heavy shell. The ghost crab (below) hides in the sand with just its eyes sticking out. It is safe from predators but can still watch for prey.

IN AND OUT OF THE WATER

Our eyes are built for one *habitat,* or kind of place. We live on land and usually go in the water for short periods of time. Some animals spend lots of time both on land and in the water. They must have eyes that work in both places.

Crocodiles sometimes hunt by floating in the water. Hippopotamuses like to cool off in the water during the heat of the day. Both of these animals have eyes near the top of their head. They can still see even when they are almost completely under water. The hippo watches for danger. The crocodile looks for prey.

The unusual fish *Anableps anableps* (ANNA–bleps) is nicknamed the "four–eyed fish." It really only has two eyes. But each eye is divided into two parts. *Anableps* often lies just at the water's surface. It can watch out for seabirds flying in the sky above it and hunt for fish in the water below it—at the same time!

Mudskippers (above) are strange fish. They spend hours out of the water sitting on the roots of mangrove trees! Their bulging, movable eyes work well underwater. Out of water, they can only see things that are very close.

WHEN YOU DON'T NEED EYES

Some animals live their whole life with only limited eyesight or none at all. There are animals that have lived for many, many generations in dark caves. Because they didn't need their eyes, these animals have gradually lost them completely. When they are very young, blind cave fish have eyes. But the eyes disappear as the fish grows older.

Moles spend most of their life tunneling through the ground, searching for food. They don't see very well. Sometimes their eyes are even covered over with skin. Moles can tell light from dark. But they rely much more on touch and smell to find prey and get around.

Earthworm eyes are just a group of light–sensitive cells covered with a jellylike substance. An earthworm can tell dark from light. It can also tell from where the light is coming. Even if an earthworm's eyes are covered, it can still sense brightness. The earthworm's whole body is light–sensitive.

We say someone is "blind as a bat." But bats aren't really blind. Some see as well as other mammals their size.